UNDERSTANDING DYSLEXIA

JESSICA RUSICK

Big Buddy Books

An Imprint of Abdo Publishing
abdobooks.com

abdobooks.com

Published by Abdo Publishing, a division of ABDO, PO Box 398166, Minneapolis, Minnesota 55439. Copyright © 2022 by Abdo Consulting Group, Inc. International copyrights reserved in all countries. No part of this book may be reproduced in any form without written permission from the publisher. Big Buddy Books™ is a trademark and logo of Abdo Publishing.

Printed in the United States of America, North Mankato, Minnesota.
052021
092021

THIS BOOK CONTAINS
RECYCLED MATERIALS

Design: Emily O'Malley, Mighty Media, Inc.
Production: Mighty Media, Inc.
Editor: Megan Borgert-Spaniol
Content Consultant: Brenda Blackmore, Special Education Director
Cover Photographs: Shutterstock Images
Interior Photographs: andresr/iStockphoto, p. 12; Shutterstock Images, pp. 4, 5, 7, 8, 9, 11, 13, 14, 15, 16, 17, 18, 19, 20, 21, 22, 23, 24, 25, 26, 27, 28, 29

Library of Congress Control Number: 2020949915

Publisher's Cataloging-in-Publication Data
Names: Rusick, Jessica, author.
Title: Understanding dyslexia / by Jessica Rusick
Description: Minneapolis, Minnesota : Abdo Publishing, 2022 | Series: Understanding disabilities | Includes online resources and index.
Identifiers: ISBN 9781532195754 (lib. bdg.) | ISBN 9781098216481 (ebook)
Subjects: LCSH: Dyslexia--Juvenile literature. | Learning disabilities--Juvenile literature. | Cognition--Social aspects--Juvenile literature. | Literacy--Social aspects--Juvenile literature. | Social acceptance--Juvenile literature.
Classification: DDC 371.914--dc23

CONTENTS

Quiz Day

It's quiz day in Kai's class. Kai copies the quiz questions from the board into his notebook. When he finishes copying, he looks around. Many classmates have already turned their quizzes in.

Kai wonders how they finished so quickly. He even wonders if he is as smart as his classmates. Kai is very smart. He just has trouble reading and writing at his classmates' pace. This is because Kai has dyslexia.

What Is Dyslexia?

Dyslexia is a learning disability. It affects the way a person's brain understands language. People with dyslexia have trouble matching letters with sounds. This makes it harder to read. It can make writing, spelling, and speaking harder too.

Dyslexia has nothing to do with being smart. Dyslexic people simply learn differently. It's important to respect people's differences. Name-calling is never okay.

Remember

People with disabilities are not **victims**. This word makes it sound like having a disability is a bad thing. But a disability is not bad. It's just a difference!

Reading can be tiring for kids with dyslexia.

Be sure to respect how a person with dyslexia chooses to **identify**. A friend with dyslexia may call herself a dyslexic person. Or she may call herself a person with dyslexia. Ask your friend which language she prefers.

Person First

Person-first language puts a person before his or her disability. People who use it believe people should not be defined by their disabilities.

I am a person with dyslexia.

Identity First

People who use **identity**-first language believe someone's disability is an important part of his or her identity. Some dyslexic people prefer to be called dyslexic.

I am a dyslexic person.

Dyslexia Symptoms

Everyone with dyslexia is different. Some people have many **symptoms**. Others have just a few. In general, dyslexia affects the way people read, write, spell, and speak.

Reading

★ Reading slowly

★ Trouble reading common words

★ Trouble sounding out new words

★ Mixing up letters that look alike, such as *b* and *d*

★ Words appear to move around or become **blurry** on the page

★ Making mistakes or taking long pauses when reading aloud

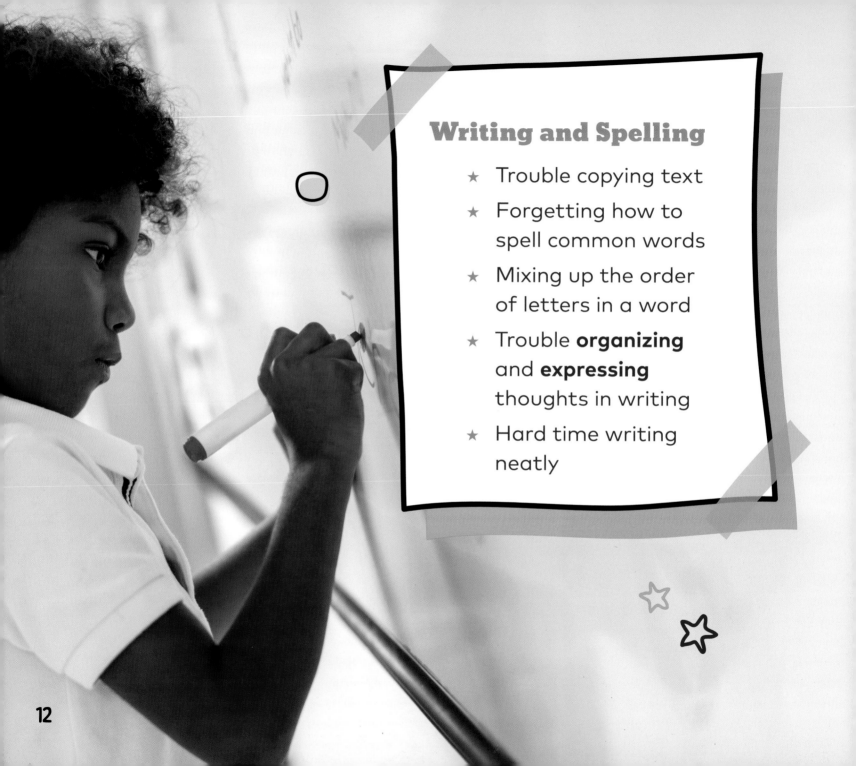

Writing and Spelling

★ Trouble copying text

★ Forgetting how to spell common words

★ Mixing up the order of letters in a word

★ Trouble **organizing** and **expressing** thoughts in writing

★ Hard time writing neatly

Speaking

- ★ **Mispronouncing** words

- ★ Mixing up words that sound alike

- ★ Trouble finding the right words to **express** a thought

13

Who Has Dyslexia?

Dyslexia can be **diagnosed** at any age. However, people are usually diagnosed as kids or young adults. Most people with dyslexia are born with it. Dyslexia is also sometimes caused by **injury** to the brain.

Dyslexia is a common learning disability. Around 80 percent of people who have trouble reading are dyslexic. Doctors believe that males and females have dyslexia at equal rates.

Dyslexia tends to run in families. This means a child is more likely to have dyslexia if her parent has it.

Dyslexia at School

School can be **stressful** for kids with dyslexia. Many school activities include reading, writing, and spelling. Dyslexic kids must give extra time and effort to these activities.

For example, dyslexic kids may have trouble taking notes in class. They may also struggle to understand what they've just read. And, they may find it **challenging** to read aloud.

To take notes, students must listen, write, and understand all at once. This learning method is not helpful for many dyslexic kids.

Certain tools and practices can help kids with dyslexia do well in school. These include:

Tutors

Tutors help dyslexic kids learn reading **strategies**. These strategies make reading easier over time.

More Time

Teachers often give kids with dyslexia more time to complete tests. That way, the kids can read and write at their own pace.

Text-to-Speech Devices

These **devices** read everything from books to websites aloud. Dyslexic kids often have an easier time understanding **information** that is read aloud to them.

Social Struggles

Kids with dyslexia may feel angry or sad that reading and writing is hard. They may even be teased by other kids. Being teased makes people feel bad about themselves.

Dyslexic kids may also have trouble finding the words they want to say. This can make it hard to talk to others. Text messaging is also **challenging**. That's because kids with dyslexia can have trouble keeping track of the meanings of **acronyms** and **abbreviations**.

If you are texting a dyslexic friend, try to keep your messages short. Spell out words instead of using abbreviations.

Being a Friend

Everyone has his or her own strengths and **challenges**. That's okay! No matter what, everyone should be treated with respect.

There are many ways to be a good friend to someone with dyslexia. Ask your friend if she wants to share what it's like having dyslexia. If she does, listen respectfully. You could also offer to help your friend with homework.

A dyslexic friend may need more time to voice his thoughts. It's important to be a kind and **patient** listener. This can help your friend feel comfortable.

Always ask whether a friend with dyslexia would like your help before you give it.

More Ways to Be a Friend

Stand Up to Bullying

Tell an adult if your friend is being teased.

Be Supportive

Tell your friend what you think she's good at.

Break it Down

People with dyslexia can find it **stressful** to get lots of **information** at once. Are you giving your friend directions? Try to break down the information into small chunks.

Strengths

Having dyslexia can be **challenging**. However, many people say their dyslexia helps them to be creative and imaginative thinkers. Dyslexic people are also known to be great problem-solvers. People with dyslexia have become successful actors, writers, scientists, and more.

Jace Norman

Jace Norman is an actor with dyslexia. He starred on the popular Nickelodeon show *Henry Danger*. Norman was bullied for his dyslexia in school. Today, Norman encourages dyslexic kids to use their strengths to be successful.

Jace Norman started acting when he was 12 years old. At 17, he started his own media company.

Golden Rules

Millions of people have disabilities. If you know someone with a disability, there may be times when you feel unsure of what to say or do. When in doubt, remember to treat others how you'd want to be treated. And, keep in mind these other golden rules:

* Accept and respect differences
* Use respectful language
* Be kind and caring

Activities

Do you have a friend who has dyslexia? Invite him or her to join you for a fun activity.

Draw, paint, or make crafts

Listen to an audio book

Play Scrabble, Words with Friends, or other simple word games

29

abbreviation—a short way to write a word.

acronym—a word made from the beginning letters of words in a phrase.

blurry—lacking a definite outline.

challenging (CHA-luhn-djing)—testing one's strengths or abilities. Something that is challenging is a challenge.

device—an object or machine that has a certain job.

diagnose (die-ugh-NOES)—to recognize something, such as a disability, by signs, symptoms, or tests.

express—to make one's feelings or thoughts known through words or actions.

identify—to say or show who someone is.

identity—the set of features and beliefs that make a person who she or he is.

information (ihn-fuhr-MAY-shuhn)—knowledge gained from learning or studying something.

injury (IHN-juh-ree)—hurt or loss received.

mispronounce—to say incorrectly.

organize—to arrange or plan something.

patient—calm and kind when waiting for something or dealing with challenges.

strategy—a careful plan.

stressful—causing stress, a feeling of worry.

symptom—a noticeable change in the normal working of the body or mind.

tutor (TOO-tuhr)—someone who teaches a student privately.

victim—someone who has been harmed by an unpleasant event.

ONLINE RESOURCES

Booklinks
NONFICTION NETWORK
FREE! ONLINE NONFICTION RESOURCES

To learn more about dyslexia, please visit **abdobooklinks.com** or scan this QR code. These links are routinely monitored and updated to provide the most current information available.

INDEX